Whoever you are, go out into the evening,
leaving your room, of which you know every bit;
your house is the last before the infinite,
whoever you are.

– Rainer Maria Rilke

McALPINE

McALPINE

Romantic Modernism

Bobby McAlpine

with Susan Sully

Principal photography by Simon Upton

New York Paris London Milan

Contents

Prelude	7
Invitatory	9
I Manse	10
Duality	**49**
II Palace	50
III Portal	70
Asylum	**85**
IV Idyll	86
V Goodness	104
Courage	**129**
VI Radiance	130
VII Joy	176
Salon	**205**
VIII Chambering	206
IX Boundless	228
Truth	**243**
X Kindness	244
XI Exuberance	254
Project Index	274
Exeunt	284
Acknowledgments	287

Come and sit next to me and I'll tell you something you may not know. If I had begun this journey by looking through the eyes of classicism or modernism, it would have been like searching for God within the confines of a single creed. A fierce romantic, I craved the rogue liberty to find an accurate voice by crossbreeding from all places and periods. Classicism and modernism are only two of them—the silver and gold crayons in the box of sixty-four colors that I've held back yet wanted to use for so long. I am now willing to embrace these doctrines more directly. Under the heading of romanticism, I can claim them as my medium to empower all else I've learned along the way. Pure classicism and modernism are daunting in their dogma. When you throw the cloak of romanticism over them, they become more subtle and even more powerful.

Prelude

They turn a house made of warm butter into something that possesses an "across the crowded room" kind of attraction, as immediate as a flash of lightning or the roll of thunder. Such a house doesn't coddle you with offerings and assets. It travels beyond romantic poetry to harness the potency of these commanding tongues. The houses in these pages are not the gentlest, but rather those that possess the most voltage. This work is about going further than poetry—it is about using all the tools I've spoken of to address some other part of you. Pure in their intent, they compose lyrics or haikus that contain within them epic novels. How do you play in five notes what previously took eleven? This is the concentrated essence that makes a star a star. It is what makes one thing stand out against the next. It is the cathedral in the house.

Invitatory

We carry love amidst all manner of contrary evidence and circumstance. How can we put our faith in one thing that seemingly contradicts another and hold both as truth? In spatial duality, inertia and ascension coexist. If only one is present, emotional dimension is lacking. This apparent contradiction speaks to us of not being any less complex than we as humans are. A simultaneous craving for order and freedom lives within us. The truth abides between them. The beautiful confrontation is where humanity lies. The nature of classicism is emblematic. It offers strict discipline and prescribed order to meandering thought. In modernism, there is freethinking rebellion. Axes and alignments follow the shape of the land or the architect's imaginings to allow the plan to take whatever form it likes. These schools seem polar opposites, but share a peculiar attraction. Conservative, liberal: they love each other. Their lessons can be combined to evolve their reach. In terms of style and philosophy, they are just two of many characters that can be married to solve a riddle. Romanticism is more akin to a dream. Free to borrow from and superimpose different epochs and cultural origins, it raids every closet and chest in your emotional house. Nothing comes close to its range and license. Like the heart, it layers time and place, free to wander and select. Turning reality into more of a sketch than a finished work of art, it is the most accurate brush for the dualities of our human construct. An unfinished painting can be infinitely more attractive than the completed work. The cartoon of a tapestry may somehow draw more affection from you than the tapestry itself. Walking you into an active process, these works of art invite you to become a player in their present and future resolution, simply by showing up.

I

As you approach the house, sound precedes it—a baritone horn cutting through fog like the signal of a ship coming to moor in this bucolic harbor. Buoyant as a waterborne vessel, the house is also grounded—a single boulder with one giant window, a geode beside the road. There is no watering down of its statement. At the same time, it invites you as a passerby to see within, offering its own vulnerability. The enormous window permits glimpses of curiosities—stone eagles standing guard and the disheveled ruins of a wing chair. It's as if you are seeing inside the mind of the house. Can you recall a time when you met someone and noticed that the most compelling feature was the light in her eyes? What you remember more than any physical trait is that flash of truth. Architecture can be used that way—to create a powerful stance in order to unravel it and make it human. It is not until you encounter

Manse

the monumental volume of the salon that you know this to be a classical container with pure axial symmetry. Perfectly balanced from front to rear and left to right, it feels taut and ready to sail. Diagonal movement comes through the appointments, energizing it and allowing it to gain even more momentum. The silence and scale of the architecture possess a watchful, generous presence that allows liberally for the skewed placement of furnishings and wandering of objects. The eccentricity of these disparate things would not be safe in a place that knew itself less than this house. Its order permits the inhabitants, human or otherwise, to be unselfconscious because the parenting is finished. They can be the children. All this makes for a place of people and talk and ideas where everybody might be a little better for the company. Can a house be a calling to come and be here and speak your mind in its presence?

The floor is a boundless cloud of marble. Like magic carpets, the slabs are large enough for you to ride on. They don't touch each other—they don't even touch the wall. They float like rafts, allowing a sense of weightlessness that takes you away from whatever reality you knew before you arrived.

There is a recurrent feeling in the house of its being a vessel—a ship, an airplane, a cathedral. It feels as if you could steer it in a straight line. But lateral information is fed into the system along the transverse axis. The house is definitely going somewhere, whispering to itself along the voyage and tending to all its parts.

The bright, white shaft of stairs could be a stalagmite or a giant crystal originating in the caves of a salt mine. It is the spiritual spine of the house—a shaft of light going from top to bottom, descending and ascending at the same rate. Laced by crisscrossing stairs, it is in full movement all the time. The warp and the weft of it are in constant motion.

A delayed discovery occurs in the lowest level of the house—the epiphany that its subterranean foundations are absolutely white and translucent. Although its chambers are excavated into the earth, the whole space possesses an antigravity quality. It feels utterly weightless. When you are held in the closeness of the architecture, you are released into light.

Duality shows up in the deliciousness of contradiction, which is really the truth about anything. It comforts us from two directions, speaking to our brains and hearts through a mussed beauty that allows us to find ourselves in it, neither in pure perfection nor lonely disarray. Duality represents this complex nature by showing us that we are not composed of a singular or linear path but of all the things that have happened along the way. It is revealed through reverential extremes, through stories, texture, and spatial dualities. When strict modernism is expressed through ravaged, porous material that is vulnerable to time, it is more relatable. When a

Duality

compressed space works hand in hand with a lofty one, we are released into a larger landscape, and ultimately, to a greater realm. Experiencing opposing thoughts or feelings simultaneously is like being held while you are falling. Light can be perceived only in the presence of darkness. If you don't befriend darkness, then you sacrifice light's wealth. When both are honored at the same rate, credence is given to who we are. Building the psyche of the human heart in three dimensions grants the heart more room. It props the door ajar so that other loves beside your own can come and join. You can signal all that gesturally in how you build and appoint a place.

II
Palace

The sound of architecture—in the assembling of a very few notes to come together in a perfect chord—sometimes includes dissonance. That sound gives it the necessary energy, the catalyst within the framework of its being. A great landscape or portrait often includes discord in its painterly palette, opening your way into it and making it more approachable.

III
Portal

Demure in the front and completely uninhibited in the back, this house illustrates that where there is virtue, there is also disobedience. Honor and respect come through conservatism, but with the liberal comes freedom and confidence. From a strong foundation, a person feels free to wander.

The word *asylum* conjures kindness. In any definition, it represents safety and protection. If you think about your day out in the world, where you've spent time among so many people and the largeness of everything, asylum is the place where you can regather yourself molecularly. A side chapel, a cabin, an alcove—it is an unwatched chamber that offers as much constant love as a parent, a friend, or a dog. This is a place that welcomes you singularly—where you and it are enough and you can always come as you are. A rhythmic returning to such sanctuary affords insights that can then be taken to the wider world. Where do you feel safe?

Asylum

In what company and context do you feel loved? A house can help solve these riddles, catching that moment in time when you find you are your best self. Here, you can safely question the boundaries of your faith and your thinking, and even the classicism you may have formulated for yourself. Architecture has the capacity to make concrete something visceral and fleeting—to take something that knows no materiality and capture it in form. By surrounding yourself with choices that have to do with lasting and things that are not going to disappoint, you foster enlightenment rather than dogma. A place of asylum prepares you to leave the better for it.

IV
Idyll

Bathing outdoors on a porch, sleeping in a bed beside windows that open to a whispering garden of palms—these are the pleasures that can be found on a private island. If you are brave enough to lose your bearings, relinquishing the facts of life for the insubstantiality of a dream, you can wake up to this unimagined bliss.

To create a safe place where we can show up as ourselves, as extraordinary and original as we are, there is room only for truth. There is no place for noise or overstimulation. We have evolved to be flowery enough in our tongues to get lost in them. What we build and how we surround ourselves can create an internal calm that allows us to deal with what matters most.

The conch-shell tease of the tower tempts you to pull the rope and sound its bell or to ascend its spiral of steps toward the limitless sky at the summit. From there, you can imagine being the sole inhabitant of the island; the sovereign of a miniature, uncharted realm; or a faithful host anticipating the arrival of a long-awaited friend.

V
Goodness

Why are we so charmed by Grant Wood's *American Gothic*? Serious, even stoic, the painting is also endearing. This landscape seemed to call for that kind of aesthetic—a weaving of crisp modernism into a familiar, white-cotton fabric. With a bit of starched-collar graphicness and self-awareness, this house is simple and honest about itself.

Sometimes, what you don't do is more important than what you do. In an odd way, this discipline sharpens us. When a house doesn't overmedicate us with its architecture, it speaks the flat, plain, honest, beautiful truth. It shares a "'tis a gift to be simple, 'tis a gift to be free" Shaker faith in the intrinsic goodness of things.

Building a house is an opportunity to restate the truth in a way that is relevant now, not mimicking what you've been handed but giving voice and shape to what lies within. Something may have germinated that needs expression—an original seed. When we can no longer digest what encircles us, how we present ourselves, or what we carry, only then is there willingness to show up in a way that is true. This is when we hunger for architecture that is eager to break rules—that has bravery and risk in its recipe. When fearlessly edited and undiluted in message or mood, architecture speaks clearly of this offering. Wide-eyed and naked to the truth

Courage

of itself, it shucks what is expected, making a singular call as if speaking only to you. Walking from your safe place to the edge and staying there, utterly vulnerable and transparent, demands courage and constancy. Think about late Elizabethan architecture, when country manors became glassier and glassier until they were fit only for summertime use. Some of the most gorgeous are like glass jewels. They don't posture and fortress themselves like a medieval thing. They possess a scale of life that is generous and celebratory, throwing the door open and freezing in that position so the tide can come in and out readily. It is a masterful way to live.

VI
Radiance

To live authentically and to build authentically is not about trying to be the same or different, but being honest about who you are. When some part of you possesses an unvoiced knowingness that is suddenly timely, it is time to push that piece forward. When I think of romantic acts, they are usually outrageous or incredibly vulnerable moments. Exotic, they can veer from apparent reality.

Where do those moments of courage come from, when you leave something off that you were about to put on out of habit? How do you show up plain to the party? This is akin to jumping off a cliff—that moment when you summon the courage to say the rawest or most blatant thing. Something in the doing of that is how you save room for otherness, when you leave some space in yourself for what you've just found.

Part of the monolithic story of this house is that the same color is used inside and out. The identical white carries over, supporting the secure feeling that you are in a solid, invincible thing. This message also comes through the consistent use of negative relief within and without, promoting the impression that you are floating, safe on a light and buoyant vessel. Vulnerability occurs only on the seaside facade.

There is a point at which the introduction of bold modernism might be an assault to delicacy. If an Italian- or Mediterranean-style building were fused with modernism, it would be strong enough to take the hit. The naiveté of colonial architecture is more fragile, but if that colonial expression is stripped down to its most basic form, it is strong enough to withstand and even welcome and embrace an infusion of modernism.

The architecture of truth knows that beauty is rooted in honest expression. It is composed not emblematically, but in faith that when all the internal parts and pieces and systems are right, it will be beautiful on the outside. What matters becomes matter. At a minimum, what you see is what you get, but within the experience of it, you find so much more.

VII
Joy

Incredibly welcoming and fast with itself, the house greets you with the open expression of a transparent inner core. Rows of plump Tuscan columns slow the conversation, offering opportunities to pause amid the quick unfolding.

Located in a traditional setting, the house not only fits in beautifully but also takes you somewhere else that is more liberal. With its high-spirited profusion of gables, the exterior hints that things are not quite as conservative as they seem. Within the forecourt, the core of the house dissolves into walls of windows, revealing the modern spirit that pervades the design.

A certain posture and a way of opening your eyes trigger sharing and truth-gathering. Taller, wider, longer than any other room in the house, the salon is often cocked toward a vast and greater landscape, both literally and figuratively. Casting vulnerability aside, it becomes emotionally immoderate, promoting intellectual travel, cerebral dance, and spiritual play. In the presence of a space that is fearless in its openness, there lies a calling to speak the truth. To the degree that it is not finishing everybody's sentences and telling everything it knows, such a place leaves room for interesting discourse. When furnishings look as if you could stir them with a stick and they would regather themselves in a way that works just fine, such rooms offer an

Salon

invitation to open-ended and surprising conversation. This is about creating a situation and then being open to where it wanders. The atmosphere of the French salons was intimate, curious, and irreverent. They took place in boudoirs where friends were invited to draw chairs and stools around the bed for conversation. When you walk that informality from the back of the house to the front, perfection is relaxed. Artifice is voted off the island. Then the salon becomes an exploratory, an observatory, a litany of 'tories—a storyatory, an ideatory, and a repository for burdens that need to be left behind. Whatever settles on you heavily is carbonated by laughter, and you might just find a place outside the false city limits to live in the mystery.

VIII
Chambering

Whereas its husk is gritty and earthen in texture and coloration, the interior is like a pearl. Its palette and material—expressed in shades of white—are absolutely modern and quiet. Fully open in relationship to the landscape, the space can also be divided by lush, enveloping fabric into cube-shaped chambers.

IX
Boundless

Part ghost, part materiality, this house appears rugged enough to have survived through centuries. It might have had other occupants, possibly livestock, or lain empty for a while, with nests built in its apertures. Thus, modernism is invited to complete a new chapter without needing to follow a trail of known residential references.

The truth is beautiful. Shifting your faith to trust in yourself, believing the instinct that who you really are is, in fact, the only thing you have to put forward—that is the best offering you have to give. A great deal of faith is involved in believing that something organized through honest and tender consideration on the inside will also be beautiful on the outside. This is about attending to the soul of the house and not putting flesh on it until the timing is right. When seen, such a house calls forth as its primary attraction what it feels like to be on the inside. It shows openly what it cannot hide. Truth becomes its new foundation. To embolden the

Truth

truth and shift your faith from style to utter statement—that is the invitation. When you wean yourself from things that aren't feeding you anymore, everything begins to look more like the fact of you. Your very gait and posture are captured by the architectural company you keep. What is no longer pertinent fades into the periphery and that which is left is refined into a chord that is the sound of you. Truth is who you want to sit next to. It's where your best friends are. It's where you feel safe. It's open enough that you feel free to wander. You know that it will always welcome you as you are and never un-love you. To abide by the truth is to live within it.

X
Kindness

A truthful house should not be composed of too many notes. It has just enough discernable structure and order for you to trust it. Its internal expression is shown on its face. Sometimes just three words are enough both to say what's really going on and to describe the place where you feel best. What are the naked facts of you? What is the root of your beauty?

XI
Exuberance

There is stature and pageantry in the salon's long run of windows, each as tall and regal in its own way as the house's parapets. Possessing the maximum amount of glazing to still remain solid, the room is more glass than wall. Its pageantry takes place amid light and air. Only the vaulted ceiling reminds you that you are in a permanent place, held up by bone.

Unlike houses where you are trying to make your way toward the backyard, this house lives forward. The entry porch, the library, and the salon spanning its center are where you want to be. The greatest asset of the house is the pastoral view from these rooms. They are designed to witness a spectacle larger than themselves.

II Usually people dress up in town and down at the coast, but this house in the Bahamas travels the opposite way. Like an immaculate acropolis on a pedestal by the sea, it possesses perfect, formal symmetry from left to right and front to back. In an almost templelike progression, wide steps rise between monumental urns to approach the terrace, where a long reflecting pool mirrors the white-on-white facade. These classical properties mature the house, taking it back in time and giving it deep roots. The exterior's almost ironic formality shifts to a more relaxed impression inside. The feeling is a little like going to a wedding at the beach in a tuxedo with bare feet. Vernacular in expression, the interior's pale plaster walls and planked ceilings appear as though bleached by sun, fading into light. At any moment, it seems the sheer wall of scrim in the dining room might be animated by an ocean breeze. Straddling a contemporary, traveled world with an ancient one, furniture and notions that are antique and modern, familiar and exotic blur time and place. Carved and gilded objects from far-flung places hint at a sunken ship's treasure story, conjuring a dreamy, utopian place. You don't know where in the world you are, only that you want to stay there longer, which is the essence of a vacation.

Palace

III With steep gables and a perfectly symmetrical facade, the street front of this house in Los Angeles's Pacific Palisades taps the iconic architectural language of America's colonial past. Addressing the traditional context of neighboring houses, it offers little foreshadowing of the almost outrageous modernism that occurs on the back. It is the perfect setup. Passing between a flanking pair of carriage houses, the path of entry is slowed by a courtyard leading toward an almost impossibly delicate pivoting door of single-leaf glass. Beyond it, a loftlike salon stretches across the rear of the house, barely contained by a wall of glass and steel. Divided panes nod to the facade's colonial styling, but the vast glass wall possesses the unhindered transparency and scale of modernism. Folding open to the landscape, its hinged panels erase the separation between indoors and out. Paralleling the windows, a span of rough-hewn posts and beams slows the release, offering a solid foundation within the ascendant space. From its conservative front to its utterly liberal back, the house invites you into a telescopic emotional sequence from being grounded to flying into space.

Portal

IV It is the ultimate dream to own a private island, an Eden in the not-yet-civilized world. This calls for a kind of housing that differs in every way from what is found in town, where you might feel the need to dress in some acceptable way. On this Bahamian islet, no opportunity was missed to evoke an otherworldly reverie. Every room inhabits its own building and each transition from one to the next transpires in open air, beneath the thatched roof of a loggia. Defined by fixed-in-place plaster drapery, the central pavilion is a theatrical piece—a stage where the true stars can be found in the surrounding world. With glass walls that retract, disappearing into the ceiling, this open-air salon is a place from which to observe and melt into sea and sky. In this remote retreat, perishable thatch abuts solid masonry and vernacular stepped-tile roofs combine with modernist devices to blur the lines between place and time. Appointed by a watchtower with a sounding bell that greets all who approach, the island is a refuge and an idyll by the sea.

Idyll

V There is a quiet reverence both in what this house does, seemingly without effort, and what it does not do. Located in a bucolic landscape in middle Tennessee, wood-planked and painted white, it is a quintessential farmhouse in the country. Marrying something as emotionally familiar as a white rural dwelling with crisp minimalism, it expresses a kind of silent modernism. Composed of more gable and wall than windows, the entry face is almost austere, with a bit of *American Gothic* stoicism. It offers no hint of the complete lucidity of the rear, which dissolves almost entirely into glass. The moment you walk through the front door, you see out transversely from an eighty-foot gallery that delivers an unimpeded view of the landscape. With a staircase thrusting its energy upward at one end and a modest stone farm sink at the other, its appointments are simultaneously resplendent and humble. Furnished with as few strokes as possible, the living room steps down from the gallery to promote the landscape beyond its walls of glass. This is a place that knows how to be quiet with itself. In its simplicity, there is boldness.

Goodness

VI Resolved simply, symmetrically, and classically, the facade of this house has an air of ambassadorial dignity. In a strong example of modernism-meets-classicism, it derives integrity both in how it is dressed and how it is not at all dressed. There is no appliqué. Where there is contour, it comes from material that has been removed, not added. Everything is expressed in negative relief. This gives the face of the house an almost monolithic expression that is masculine in its strength, but feminine in some of its detail, including three softly shaped windows recessed above the entrance. Knowing that the house would show its greatest luminosity along the waterfront facade, where it becomes a full-on glass palace, the entry face is slow to give that asset away. Utterly transparent on the rear, it resolves itself to become a lit lantern at night for anyone on the water to see. Billowing upward like sails lifted by the wind, repetitive plaster vaults ripple across the ceiling of the salon and cascade downward in the hall, never allowing you to forget this is a house on the water in the breeze.

Radiance

VII Rather than an academic study in style, this house is a beautiful white-on-white bloom, both joyous and regal in expression. In shape, the parapets surrounding it on all four sides might be called Cape Dutch or Flemish in silhouette, but in fact, they are neither. They are glad hands like those of an animated conversationalist who gestures and waves as he talks. Equally expressive dormer windows with wide shutters and animated roof caps issue a "come hither" invitation from between the two front parapets, drawing you in to the forecourt. Resembling a celebratory pavilion with glazed walls that are honest and forthcoming in their transparency, the inner face of the house lets down its guard and invites you to do the same. Traditional with its loggia of Tuscan columns, the central facade is also modern in expression with a long, tall curtain wall of glass. Rotating on a central pivot, the front door opens to a broad salon that duplicates this progression with rows of columns framing a rear wall made sheer by mullioned glass. Modern in its play of white and gray, the interior relies on the surrounding wood and plaster for texture and warmth. Here, the conversation is safe and quiet. Exuberant on the outside, with shapely parapets unfurling like a flower's petals, the rooms within are still.

Joy

VIII Multicloistered, this gregarious house rambles to stay thin and bright. Rich in sequence and chambering, it wraps itself around itself, making rooms of gardens and gardens of rooms. More place than object or statement, it defies any singular description to become more of a feeling. Earthen on one face and ascendant on the other, it starts its story slightly underground, with strong, impenetrable walls pressed into the terrain. The opposite side stands atop a hill, overlooking the New England countryside through the pillars of a porch that flies freely through space. Without accompanying any building, this span simply follows the horizon like a bridge—a light-seeking, light-generating experience. A crucial double message is being offered here—that you are safe and held while also being shown and invited into largeness. This experience is echoed within, where three enormous box-bay windows with hundreds of panes of glass appoint three tall, draped chambers. These illumine a long walking axis that is the sole means of traversing the house. Its progression through rooms layered by curtains invites you to pause and simply be there, as you might in a gallery, or to walk on through. By the time you travel from one end to the other, you are washed over by light, stature, and the beauty of the landscape.

Chambering

IX Located on a hillside with panoramic views of Virginia farmland, this site's engagement with the world demanded a house with huge apertures and a loftlike interior for which there was simply no domestic model. The context of old farm structures dotting the landscape further released the house from residential language, allowing its design to drift toward that of a building that might once have been a part of agrarian industry—a stable or wagon house or barn. It looks as though it has a past, but not as a dwelling. Composed of stone, slate, and steel, the house feels more permanent and invincible than the lovely but perishable carpenter-built structures around it. Its weightiness instills confidence, stability, and trust that, as the seat of this property, it will always be there for this family. Although its walls are rugged in material, they are carbonated by glass. The clarity of the windows satisfies the need to witness what lies around the house, away from it, and above it. Seeming contradictions, transparency and solidity are actually beautiful complements. The sheer and the opaque are great friends to openness. One grounds the other.

Boundless

X Standing at the intersection of a broad boulevard and a narrow lane in the Belle Meade neighborhood of Nashville, Tennessee, this house is afforded the luxury of two facades. On the boulevard, an elevation with Georgian symmetry opens to its surroundings with a host of floor-length windows. The odd thing is that there is no front door here, only windows large enough to walk through that seem to open toward the terrace rather than recede into the house. The act of entering through the side of the house lends an intimate, casual feeling to the otherwise classical English design. The glad shaping of the gable and textured, painted brick of the entry face lend kindness to its demeanor. Befriended by the gesture of coming in through a side door nestled beside the broad chimney and Flemish parapet, you enter as if family or trusted guest. The massive chimney wall piques your curiosity, promising that there is something wonderful on the other side. It sets up the powerful moment of entering the great salon broadside, encountering its double mantelpieces and floor-to-ceiling windows and being released back out to the landscape.

Kindness

XI   Exuberant and crossbred, this house in Birmingham, Alabama, engages Dutch and Elizabethan influences to create an aesthetic that amplifies their openness and animation. Highly visible from a well-traveled thoroughfare along a golf course, the dwelling is unusual in that it lives forward to the street rather than away from it. With two wings forming a U-shaped embrace, it reaches out to all who pass by. Knowing that it is being looked at, it stands there to greet you with tall, curvaceous parapets like those lining the canals of Amsterdam. These celebrate their place in the world. Spanning the space between them, a long retinue of windows echoes the transparent walls of Elizabethan manors, which freed from the fortressing of medieval architecture embraced the light. The inhabited spaces of this house are right there to be seen and have a great deal of energy pulsing outward. There is an honesty and kindness to this house, not only in its palette but also in its messaging and posture. It is an important achievement when architecture can find its beauty through vulnerability.

Exuberance

Exeunt

On Intimacy by Bobby McAlpine

Where were you when you felt safe, known, and clever?

Where were you when you could not stay too long, being held in time and invitation ever tighter, ever expanding?

What lap were you in when wonderment was backed by love, where you were seen and heard and invited into compression, kind light, and warmth?

I crave the feeling, all roomy and small, the heart's very next containment just outside my chest, open caged.

Where once I was furniture, now I am rooms.

When you spot me, you know me and curious to know more, you wade into me like a few cocktails.

The value of this realm is the freeing of you to larger landscape.

The heart expanded becomes the truth of you in finest share and offering.

It is the embodiment of your consideration when all characters are gathered and walked to your den to meet the corners of you, then brought forward from the back rows into light.

Here is the beginning of a place like no other in this world.

It is the inclusion of your timidity and longing, of all the characters within you who have never spoken.

It is as rich and naked as facts.

It is the truth of you.

Unbearable to an imposter, it is elixir to one's long, lonely search.

Here, permission flows and walls dissolve.

Here, it looks just like your life.

It is from here, having been corralled just so, that you will evolve to walk toward ever-increasing measure.

Here, you may rhythmically return, for it is closest to the well of you.

Meet me there in dappled light where gravity is stirred by promise in that particular pairing of inertia and ascension.

When the dust settles on all agitation and misfit, when the garment needs no tugging or pulling, when the marbles find their recesses, and noise subsides,

the invitation can be heard, wonderment comes, and traveling begins.

In this place and moment, we know we are loved and loosely held by it.

We wear it like a shawl and, both cradled and charged, ponder larger realms.

Certain architecture, parent, or friend affords this state.

Here, generosity is born and benevolence roots.

What is distant and close before us is invited in to pass through and finally shell behind us,

first one, then another, till we are one with what was once apart from us.

As we feel safe to reach outward and long, these alcoves and recesses, ledges and compressions hold us two-thirds of the way, the exact length of a successful cantilever.

Now house becomes metaphor for love.

It is here, through repetition of leaving the lap to walk and rhythmically return, that faith is born.

From here, you pass from in to out until you become more akin to doorway than chamber.

Treasure gets dragged across in both directions in ebb and flow and evidence washes over until you are polished to refine the light of you in all your attractions.

Then, colored and flavored by practice of choices and patterns of decision,

all comes to resemble the landscape of home.

In my life, I have known a few thin places.

Be they wood, stone, or person, they calm and quiet me, calling forth what is beyond me and what is deeply back-rowed within me to meet and be freed by reflection.

Recognizing themselves in this or that, these disparate characters find a foothold to stand and claim and speak their kindred evidence.

I know this place when I see it, cherish it when I'm in it, and can make it when I'm asked.

It is what I am given to.

The vision, passion, and talents of many people come together in the houses represented in these pages. None would exist without the seed of inspiration planted by the homeowners, who dreamed of these houses long before their foundations were laid. Through the work and dedication of my partners, Greg Tankersley and Ray Booth, and the McALPINE staff in Nashville, Atlanta, New York, and Montgomery, these dreams were brought into reality. This work could not have been achieved without our talented team, also including interior designers Susan Ferrier (*Radiance*, *Chambering*, *Boundless*), Meg Joannides (*Portal*), Teresa Palmer (*Goodness*), Isabelle Dreher, Elizabeth Dreher Lawrence, and Mila Dreher Hirsch (Exuberance); landscape architects Mike Kaiser (*Manse*, *Idyll*, *Goodness*, *Radiance*), Ben Page (*Palace*, *Kindness*), Gavin Duke (*Joy*), Christine London (*Portal*), Kathryn Herman (*Chambering*), and Thomas Woltz (*Boundless*); landscape gardeners

Acknowledgments

Paul Dreher, Paul Dreher Jr., and Susan Neylan Dreher (*Exuberance*); and countless master artisans, craftsmen, and builders. The creation of a book also required the collective vision, skill, and dedication of many people. The beauty of these pages owes much to the work of principal photographer, Simon Upton, and of photographers Bill Abranowicz, Roger Davies, and Peter Vitale. Kris Kendrick helped with our vast photo library and so much more, and Isabel Parra offered her assistance, keen eye, and lovely spirit on locations. Richard Norris's art direction and editorial oversight ensured that every detail of the book was realized with care and a commitment to perfection. Coauthor Susan Sully brought insight and precision to her treatment of the text. Gratitude is also offered to graphic designers Sam Shahid and Matthew Kraus, book consultants Jill Cohen and Lizzy Hyland, and Rizzoli International Publications senior editor Philip Reeser and publisher Charles Miers.

First published in the United States of America in 2023 by
Rizzoli International Publications, Inc.
300 Park Avenue South
New York, New York 10010
rizzoliusa.com

Publisher: Charles Miers
Senior Editor: Philip Reeser
Production Manager: Alyn Evans
Design Coordinator: Olivia Russin
Copy Editor: Elizabeth Smith
Proofreader: Sarah Stump
Managing Editor: Lynn Scrabis

Book design by Sam Shahid and Matthew Kraus, Shahid / Kraus & Company

Developed in collaboration with Jill Cohen Associates, LLC

Copyright © 2023 by McAlpine Tankersley Architecture, P.C.
Text by Bobby McAlpine with Susan Sully

All photographs © Simon Upton except for images in the following chapters:
Portal: Roger Davies; *Idyll*: William Abranowicz; *Boundless*: Peter Vitale

Excerpt of poem on page 1 is from *Rainer Maria Rilke: Fifty Selected Poems with Translations by C. F. MacIntyre* (Berkeley: University of California Press, 1940).

All rights reserved. No part of this publication may be reproduced, stored in a retrieval system, or transmitted in any form or by any means, including photocopying, recording, or other electronic or mechanic methods, without the prior written permission of the publisher.

ISBN: 978-0-8478-6947-3
Library of Congress Control Number: 2022941815

2023 2024 2025 2026 / 10 9 8 7 6 5 4 3 2 1

Printed in Italy

United States federal regulations governing the trade and ownership of animal-derived objects are under constant review and subject to change at any time. The employees of McAlpine are respectful of these laws and are particularly conscious of the ethical treatment of all animals. Some animal-derived objects displayed in the interiors of this book are antiques that date back decades or more and were acquired from licensed dealers. The decorative rhinoceros on page 30 is made of resin.